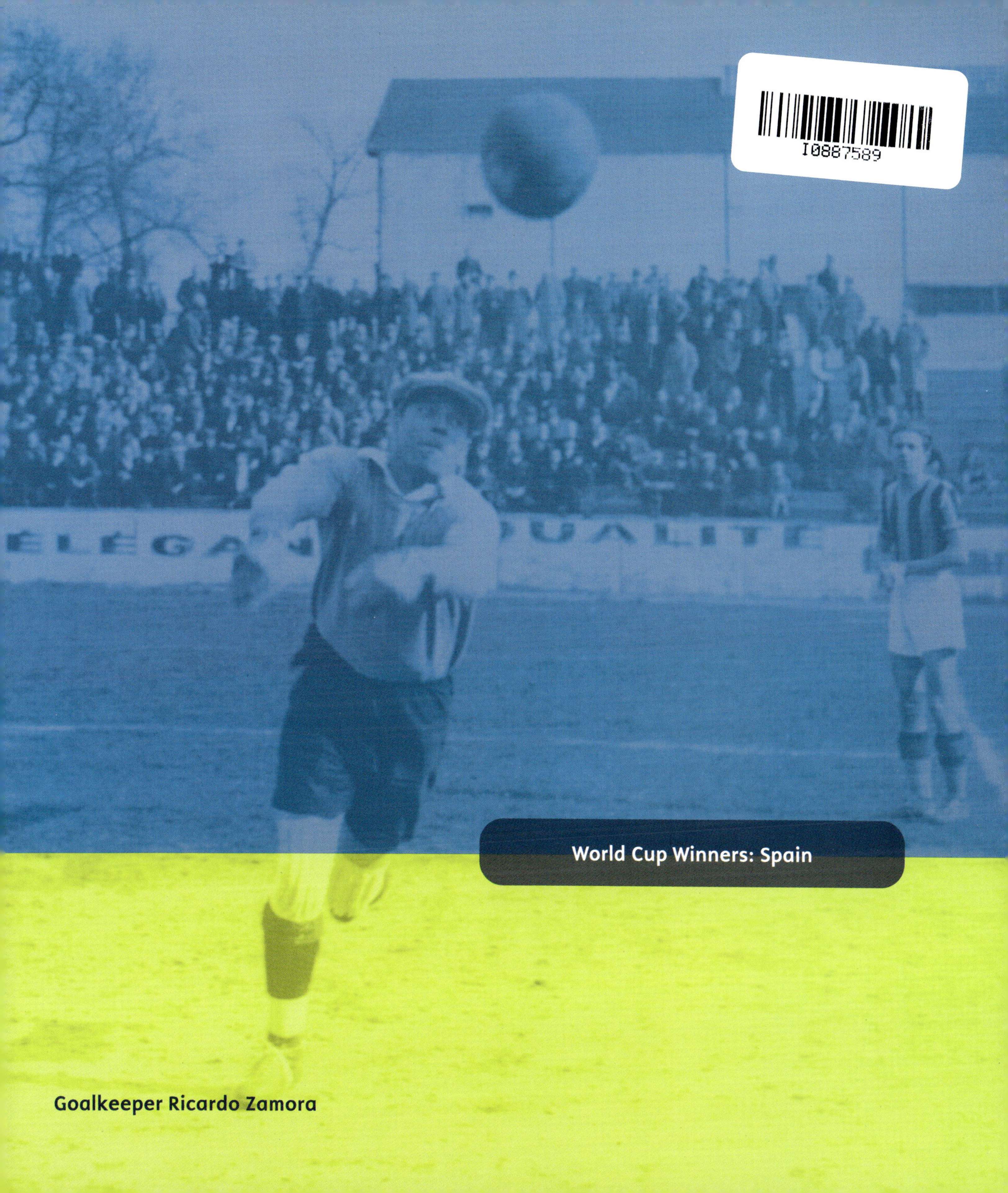

World Cup Winners: Spain

Goalkeeper Ricardo Zamora

Defensive midfielder Rodri

WORLD CUP WINNERS

SPAIN

JASON OLSON

CREATIVE SPORTS

CREATIVE EDUCATION / CREATIVE PAPERBACKS

Published by Creative Education and Creative Paperbacks
P.O. Box 227, Mankato, Minnesota 56002
Creative Education and Creative Paperbacks are imprints of
The Creative Company
www.thecreativecompany.us

Book design by Blue Design (www.bluedes.com)

Images by Getty Images/Alex Livesey - Danehouse, 2, Alex Livesey - FIFA, 3, 10, Clive Mason, 5, JEFF PACHOUD, 16, Laurence Griffiths, 6, Marvin Ibo Guengoer - GES Sportfoto, cover, 7, Matthew Ashton, 15, sampics, 19, STAFF/AFP, 1, Stu Forster, 20; Pexels/Miguel Cuenca, 9; Wikimedia Commons/Clément Bucco-Lechat, 4, public domain, 12, 24
Every effort has been made to contact copyright holders for material reproduced in this book. Any omissions will be rectified in subsequent printings if notice is given to the publisher.

Names: Olson, Jason, 1981– author.
Title: Spain / Jason Olson.
Description: Mankato, Minnesota : Creative Education and Creative Paperbacks, [2026] | Series: Creative sports: World Cup winners | Includes index. | Audience: Ages 7–10 years | Audience: Grades 2–3 | Summary: "With a FIFA World Cup and several major European titles to boast, Spain may be Europe's most successful 21st-century national soccer team. This elementary title follows "La Roja" as it seeks another FIFA World Cup"– Provided by publisher.
Identifiers: LCCN 2024046141 (print) | LCCN 2024046142 (ebook) | ISBN 9798889896043 (lib. bdg.) | ISBN 9781682777701 (paperback) | ISBN 9798889896845 (ebook)
Subjects: LCSH: Roja (Soccer team)–History–Juvenile literature. | Soccer teams–Spain–History–21st century–Juvenile literature. | Soccer—Spain—History—Juvenile literature. | World Cup (Soccer—Juvenile literature. | European Championship (Soccer tournament)–Juvenile literature. | Summer Olympics–Juvenile literature.
Classification: LCC GV943.6.R54 047 2026 (print) | LCC GV943.6.R54 (ebook) | DDC 796.334/660946—dc23/eng/20241214
LC record available at https://lccn.loc.gov/2024046141
LC ebook record available at https://lccn.loc.gov/2024046142

Printed in India

Midfielder Xavi

Midfielder Xabi Alonso

CONTENTS

Home of the Team

Spain is a large country in western Europe. It spans an important area between Europe and Africa. It's known for traditions like flamenco dancing and bullfighting.

The Spanish love to cheer on their national soccer team. It's one of the few teams to have won the World Cup. The World Cup is a worldwide soccer tournament. Countries make teams of their best players. Every four years, they compete to become world champion.

Striker David Villa

SPAIN

Team Traditions

The Spain national team is called "La Roja" ("The Red") or "La Furia Roja" ("The Red Fury"). It plays powerful, aggressive soccer. Its playstyle is also known as "tiki-taka" for grouping short passes together to build an attack. The team celebrates its wins with a parade through the streets of the capital Madrid. Spain plays **rivals** Portugal in "The Iberian Derby" and Italy in "The Mediterranean Derby."

The Spain national team, 1920

Team History

Spain did not form a national team until 1920. The team took part in the Olympics, finishing second. Spain won its first major title in the 1964 European Championship, defeating the Soviet Union 2–1. It went on to finish fourth at the 1950 World Cup.

Spain won the World Cup in 2010. It defeated the Netherlands 1–0 in the final. Andrés Iniesta scored the winner in extra time—in the 116th minute! It's the latest winning goal in a World Cup final.

The 2010 World Cup took place in South Africa. Spain was the first European team to win the trophy outside Europe. Goalkeeper Iker Casillas won the **Golden Glove**.

Midfielder Andrés Iniesta

Midfielder Xavi

Many soccer experts say Spain is "the team of the 21st century." Its golden generation won three European Championships—in 2008, 2012, and 2024. Spain holds the European title record. It was named Team of the Year every year from 2008 to 2013.

Team Stars

Spain has had many stars in its history. Sergio Ramos scored 23 goals in a record 180 **caps**. Iniesta is one of the best midfielders and a runner-up for the **Ballon d'Or**. Iniesta, Xavi, and Xabi Alonso are known for working together in midfield.

Centre-back Sergio Ramos (left)

Winger Lamine Yamal

David Villa is Spain's all-time leading scorer, with 59 goals in 98 caps. He was the top scorer at the 2008 European Championship. Villa was runner-up for the **Golden Boot** at the 2010 World Cup.

In 2024, Lamine Yamal became the youngest player to play and score in a European Championship. It was just before his 17th birthday! Rising stars like Yamal hope to bring another World Cup to Spain soon.

About the Spain National Team

First year: 1920

Team colors: red, yellow, dark blue, black

Home stadium: various (including Santiago Bernabéu, Metropolitano, Benito Villamarín, and Camp Nou)

WORLD CUP VICTORY:

2010, 1–0 over the Netherlands

WEBSITE:

https://rfef.es/en

Glossary

Ballon d'Or — an award given every year to the world's best soccer player

cap — an official match played for a national soccer team

Golden Boot — an award given to the player with the most goals in a tournament

Golden Glove — an award given to the best goalkeeper in a tournament

rival — a team that plays extra hard against another team

The Spain national team, 1950

Index